Only Silly Things!

A Collection of Hilarious Poems

Arshia Singh

Made with ❤ on the BookLeaf Publishing Platform
www.bookleafpub.in
www.bookleafpub.com

Dedication

To the ones who never stop laughing, even when the jokes are bad; and that is my family. This book is for you.

Preface

There is joy and laughter in everyone's life, even if you don't realize it. So, this is why I wrote this book – to get you laughing uncontrollably, or even get the slightest of a smile on your faces. Some of these poems will make you laugh, others might make you smile a little, and a few could leave you wondering whether you are even reading the right book! But that is the joy of humour – it's all about embracing the chaos and finding the funny in the ridiculous. So, sit back, grab a cup of coffee if you want to, and enjoy the ride!

Acknowledgements

I would like to express my heartfelt gratitude towards BookLeaf for publishing my poetry book. Also to my friends and family for their unwavering support and encouragement throughout the journey; especially Hunnarr Sareen, a friend of mine, for her support and ideas for the poems. Lastly, I thank you, readers for even smiling while reading this silly collection of poems. (And even if you didn't, I still appreciate that.)

Random Things

Random things popping in my head,
Cats, dogs, and even bread!
A boy who is so clumsy is after,
Random people full of laughter!

Next is a bunch of parallel lines,
Police officers collecting taxes and fines.
Look, the horse just jumped over the fence,
Yes, I know these things make no literal sense!

I'll try not to think about random things,
But here we go again - a bunch of rings.
I'll end this one with fandom,
But now I ran out of things random!

What if Your Name

What if your name,
wasn't the same?
What if it was 'Cow',
things won't be normal like now.

What if your name was 'Hay',
that you would never want to say.
Imagine your name being 'Loo',
everyone would really hate you.

Imagine a bad name you had to bear,
you would not get love or care.
So be happy with your name,
and never think of changing it again.

I'm at the Circus

I'm at the circus,
This is really not fun.
Clowns are all around,
Oh my, I'm really done.

They can balance things so well,
This is too much to digest.
Oh, this is really bad,
Worse than not getting enough rest.

Do the gymnasts even have bones?
It doesn't seem so.
These animals terrify me,
That one's near me, oh no!

I don't really think,
A circus is a good place.
I am so terrified,
You wouldn't want to see my face!

Did You Know?

Did you know?
It was once in this world that monsters ruled!
I know it looks fake,
But it really is true!

Did you know?
It was once in this world that kings had to clean!
I didn't believe it myself at first,
Very fake it seems.

Did you know?
It was once in this world that robots were called "fools"!
Isn't it surprising?
These facts are so cool!

I know you are amazed,
"I wish I knew this before!" you say with a sigh.
But whatever I told you,
It was all a lie!

The Cat Thought it was a Whale

The cat thought it was a whale,
That was a total disaster - an epic fail.
"Whales like me are so cool,"
Said that cat, it is such a fool.

It walked down to the sea.
"Time to dive, I'm ready!
There I go, this is going to be so fun!
Help! I can't swim, I want to run!"

"I'm a whale, I am supposed to swim," the cat said with a
sigh.
"I don't think I'm a whale, this must be a lie!"
The goat said, "It is a lie, you are not a whale, you are a
cow,"
The cat said, "What? Are you serious right now?"

The Worst Superhero

I'm the superhero that you'll never need,
I'm like a plant, but with no seeds.
I can fly, but only an inch from the ground,
I can make a noise, but it's barely a sound.

I always try to save the day,
I want to help, but I can't really find the way.
I could turn invisible, not stay in sight,
But only for a second, yes that's right.

Don't expect much from me,
I can't give you any guarantee.
I must be the worst superhero,
Or maybe just a weirdo!

The Moon was Tired

The moon was tired,
It needed a break.
It wanted to rest,
And have some cake.

"The stars are enough,
I don't need to shine.
If we hire more stars,
Everything will be just fine!"

So it called the stars,
And gave them a raise.
Then, it hired more stars,
To take the moon's place!

The new stars twinkled,
All shiny and bright,
But the moon just slept,
Out of sight!

My Mother Won't Listen to Me

My mother won't listen to me,
She's busy playing video games.
She's got a controller in her hand,
And her character is totally lame.

She's always on her phone,
Scrolling Instagram for fame,
She thinks the more she scrolls,
The more she'll make her name.

She never wants to work,
Says, "Who needs that stress?"
She thinks that posting videos,
Will bring her fame and success.

She never notices my work,
What am I wearing? It's hard to say.
But she'll watch the new web series,
And finish it all in one day.

The Broken Umbrella

Oh no! It's raining,
I need to go visit my friend.
Let me get that umbrella,
Before I get soaked and drenched!

I can't find it,
Where is it hiding now?
I put it in my room,
It just disappeared, how?

Finally—I found it,
But guess what? It's broken. It really is true!
I guess I'll have to run to her place,
And that's totally not cool!

The Alarm Clock is Done

The alarm clock is done,
Trying to wake up a lazy person is no fun.
It rings and rings, doesn't stop,
But the snooze button makes it a total flop.

With all its might, it screams,
While the lazy sleeper just dreams.
It rang so loud, it might just fall,
But the sleeper hears nothing at all.

"I give up," it said with a sigh.
"This person is too sleepy, that's no lie."
The sleeper finally woke up with a yawn,
"Guess I'll start the day now," but the clock was gone.

The Teacher isn't Here

The teacher isn't here,
We're free for the day!
No homework to complete,
No instructions to obey.

We will gossip and giggle,
And there's no one to fear.
Who's going to stop us?
We'll keep having fun, my dear!

We'll go crazy and make noise,
Without any shame.
But if she comes back,
We won't act the same!

I am Bored

I'm bored,
I don't know what to do.
What game should I play?
I have no clue.

Books are too boring and long,
Games are too hard.
Chess has too much to focus on,
Harder than playing with a deck of cards.

Maybe I could watch a movie,
But no—it's too slow.
Social media is fun,
But it's full of things I don't know.

Maybe I should just give up,
There's nothing to entertain me.
I should take a nap,
And just let it be.

My Uncle Sent Me a Mystery Box

My uncle sent me a mystery box,
It could be a diamond, or just some rocks.
An expensive showpiece, or maybe an Apple watch I'll find,
I'm so curious to know what's hiding inside!

I thought there would be some money,
But what a fool I was, it really is funny!
I opened it quickly, thinking of a car,
But my expectations just went too far!

I looked inside, my eyes wide full of glee,
But what did I see?
The box was empty - nothing inside,
I said, "Fine, but not next time!"

How My Sister Lost her Brain

My sister was jumping and dancing in the rain,
She didn't realize she had lost her brain.
She was just enjoying her day,
Couldn't see it as it slipped away.

She searched the garden, searched all around,
But her brain was nowhere to be found.
She searched in the house, everywhere it could go,
But where was it? She didn't know.

Then, a thought struck her like a flash of light,
"Perhaps it is hidden from me, out of sight!".
She stopped looking for it, went to get some fresh air,
For now, she had realized her brain was never really
there!

My Dog

My dog is such a fool,
It's only known for being cute.
It can't speak,
Or even wear a suit.

I took it to the pool,
It couldn't even swim.
It's so hairy,
And it doesn't want a trim.

It's just a dog,
Might not be so smart.
But one thing I'm sure about,
It is kind, it has a heart.

It's the Holidays

It's the holidays,
We will have fun!
Do whatever you want,
There's no stress, no tension!

We will go shopping and to the game zone,
Then we'll win every game and say "Yay!"
And most importantly,
We'll sleep all day.

We'll sing till we're tired,
Maybe dance on the floor,
And when it's all over,
We'll do it some more!

Everyone Is Hungry

Everyone is hungry,
And there's nothing to eat.
I checked the fridge,
There are no treats!

No chips, no cheese,
No fruit and no meat.
We sit down as we starve,
And beg for something to eat.

But then I call out,
"Let's order some food, that would be cool!"
But no one knew how to,
Sitting like a fool.

The Boastful Spider

I'm the best at making webs,
No one else can match my threads.
My designs are bold and fine,
Others fail, but I shine.

The contest began and I'm ready to do my best,
But guess what? My web's a mess!
I couldn't stand still, I tripped and fell,
Oh my! That didn't go well.

I thought I'd win, but now I know,
I'm not the best, my skills are low.
I'll do it again, I'll try my best,
But for now, I'll just take some rest!

Where Did the Cake Go?

It's my birthday,
I'll eat so much cake,
Cake gives me so much joy,
The feeling that I can't fake.

Cream so tasty, layers so tall,
I dreamed of devouring it all!
But now that cake so pretty,
Disappeared—what a pity!

I looked in the fridge, stared at the floor,
Even checked the pantry door.
I asked everybody, even my cat,
"Do you know where the cake is?" But they all stared
back.

I couldn't find where it is,
And that is something that I really hate.
But then I looked forward,
And realized the cake was on my plate!

My "Fun Day" at the Beach

I'm at the beach,
I got to enjoy today.
The sun shines bright,
And the waves totally slay!

I built a castle, standing tall,
Had a meal, but dropped it all.
But then my dog—should I really tell?
Well, just know there was a really bad smell!

I tried to act like it's okay, tried to stay cool,
But my dog was standing there, looking like a fool!
Still, I laughed, what else could I do?
Best beach day...with a side of poo!

I Lost my Socks

I was all ready, ready to go.
But something felt off, I didn't know.
I checked all around, and what did I see?
My socks were gone! They just vanished mysteriously.

I searched every corner,
Here and there.
In the cupboard, on the ground,
In the washing machine, even in my hair!

Turns out, they're hiding, playing a game,
Probably even calling me names!
But I'll find them, sooner or later,
Unless they're on a vacation to the moon's crater!